CONTENTS

how2become

A Traffic Officer
The Insider's Guide

Orders: Please contact How2become Ltd, Suite 2,
50 Churchill Square Business Centre, Kings Hill,
Kent ME19 4YU.

Telephone: (44) 0845 643 1299 - Lines are open Monday to
Friday 9am until 5pm. Fax: (44) 01732 525965. You can also
order via the e mail address info@how2become.co.uk.

ISBN: 978-1-907558-10-8

First published 2010

Copyright © 2010 how2become Ltd.

Typeset for How2become Ltd by Good Golly Design,
Canada, goodgolly.ca

Printed in Great Britain for How2become Ltd by Bell & Bain
Ltd, 303 Burnfield Road, Thornliebank, Glasgow G46 7UQ.

WELCOME

Welcome to how2become a *Traffic Officer: The Insider's Guide*. This guide has been designed to help you prepare for, and pass the Traffic Officer selection process. As you can imagine, the selection process to join is highly competitive. There are very few jobs, yet the competition is fierce. You could view this as a worrying fact, or alternatively you could take the view that you are determined to be one of the few people who manages to pass the selection process and realise their dream of becoming a Highways Agency Traffic Officer (HATO). Armed with this insider's guide, you have certainly taken the first step to passing the selection process.

The guide itself has been divided into useful sections to make it easier for you to prepare for each stage. Read each section carefully and take notes as you progress. Don't ever give up on your dreams; if you really want to become a Traffic Officer then you can do it. The way to approach the selection process is to embark on a programme of 'in-depth' preparation, and this guide will show you exactly how to do that. The HATO selection process is not easy to pass. Unless, that is, you put in plenty of preparation. Your preparation

 how2become

must be focused in the right areas, and be comprehensive enough to give you every chance of success. This guide will teach you how to be a successful candidate. The way to pass the selection process is to develop your own skills and experiences around the assessable competencies that are required to perform the role. Many candidates who apply to join will be unaware that the competencies even exist. As you progress through this guide you will find that these important elements of the Traffic Officer's role will form the foundations of your preparation. So, the first step in your preparation and before we go any further, is to get hold of a copy of the competencies. They will usually form part of your application pack but if they don't, you can obtain a copy of them by visiting the Highways Agencies website at www.highways.gov.uk. If you need any further help with any elements of the HATO selection process, including the interview, then we offer a wide range of products to assist you. These are all available through our online shop www.how2become.co.uk. We also run a one-day intensive Traffic Officer course. Details are available at the website www.TrafficOfficerCourse.co.uk.

Once again, thank you for your custom and we wish you every success in your pursuit of a career as a Traffic Officer. Work hard, stay focused and be what you want.

Best wishes,

The how2become team

The How2become team

PREFACE

By Author Richard McMunn

In 1993 I joined the Fire Service after serving four years in the Fleet Air Arm branch of the Royal Navy. After spending 16 successful years in the Fire Service, I decided to set up my own business and teach people like you how to prepare for a specific job. I have passed many different job applications and interviews during my life and I have also sat on the opposite side of the interview desk. Therefore, I have plenty of experience and knowledge that I will be sharing with you throughout this guide.

Throughout my career and working life I have always found that if I apply myself, and focus on the job in hand, then I will be successful. It is a formula that I have stuck with for many years, and it has always served me well. This kind of approach is one that I want to teach you over the forthcoming pages of this guide, and I hope that you will use my skills and knowledge to help you achieve the same levels of success that I have enjoyed. Personally, I do not believe in luck when applying for jobs. I believe those candidates who successfully pass the HATO selection process do so

because they thoroughly deserve it. They have prepared well and they have worked hard in order to improve their skills and knowledge.

I have always been a great believer in preparation. Preparation was my key to success, and it is also yours. Without the right level of preparation you will be setting out on the route to failure. The Highways Agency is very hard to join, simply because there are very few vacancies. When they do arise, there are always plenty of applicants. However, follow the steps that I have compiled within this guide then you will increase your chances of success dramatically. Remember, you are learning how to be a successful candidate, not a successful Traffic Officer! The Highways Agency, like many other public services, has changed a great deal over the years and even more so in how it assesses potential candidates for Traffic Officer positions. Before you apply to join the Highways Agency you need to be fully confident that you are capable of providing a very high level of customer care to the people whom you'll be serving. If you think you can do it, and you can rise to the challenge, then you just might be the type of person they are looking for. As you progress through this guide you will notice that the assessable competencies required to become a Traffic Officer are a common theme. You **must** learn these competencies, and also be able to demonstrate them throughout the selection process, if you are to have any chance of successfully passing the selection process.

Those candidates who make little or no effort to demonstrate the competencies will fail; it's as simple as that.

Richard McMunn

Richard McMunn

CHAPTER I
INTRODUCTION

One of the most important aspects of any selection process is your ability and motivation to prepare. If you are serious about becoming a Traffic Officer, and you meet the minimum eligibility requirements, then there is nothing stop you achieving your goal. Yes you may have to wait a while before vacancies are advertised, but if are prepared to work hard at the selection process then there is no reason why you can't succeed. Make sure you do everything possible to learn about the Highways Agency and in particular the role of a Traffic Officer; after all, this is how you'll be assessed. Learn and understand the selection process and prepare fully for every stage.

The Highways Agency usually advertises Traffic Officer vacancies through their website, which can be found at the following website:

http://www.highways.gov.uk

From this website you can sign up for job alerts, download an application pack and also read more about the selection process and what it involves. It is important from the offset to understand what the Highways Agency is all about. Again, from the above website you can find out this information so make sure you take the time to read it. Preparation is everything during your pursuit to becoming a Traffic Officer.

THE JOB DESCRIPTION

Before we go any further with this guide, it is important to make reference to the job description (JD). The Highways Agency will be looking for successful candidates to demonstrate some experience of the different aspects that cover the JD. For example, part of the Traffic Officers duties will include having an ability to provide a high level of customer care. Therefore, it is not unreasonable for the Highways Agency to expect you to have some previous experience in this field. Let us take a look at a sample job description which is centred around the role of a Traffic Officer:

SAMPLE JOB DESCRIPTION

Highways Agency Traffic Officer (HATO)

This is a safety critical role due to fact that successful candidates will be required to work on the major roads, motorway networks and also be required to deal with road users.

MAIN RESPONSIBILITIES OF THE TRAFFIC OFFICER ROLE

- Provide an on-road presence and resource which effectively supports the Highways Agency's Network Operator Role.

- Manage Road Traffic Collisions (RTC's)

- Reduce congestion following on-road incidents
- Facilitate the removal of damaged/ broken down and abandoned vehicles
- Remove debris, foreign objects and animals from the carriageway
- To improve road safety for all road users
- Undertaking high visibility patrols
- Set up and manage road closures
- Escort high-risk vehicles and loads
- Improve journey time for all road users
- Monitor the road networks and provide reports
- Provide a high level of customer service and care
- Support special events as and when required
- Work with other agencies and provide support to the Police
- Attend legal proceedings and provide evidence in court as a witness as and when required
- Providing first aid when first on the scene at an accident

ACTION POINTS

1. Visit the Highways Agency website and download a copy of the role profile for a Traffic Officer. Learn the role carefully and be capable of reciting it at interview.

2. Make a note of the assessable competencies and write down your skills, experiences and qualifications that match them. You will be required to provide evidence of

how you match each and every one of the competencies during the selection process.

3. Try to think of experiences you have already gained in life that match the role profile. For example, if one of the competencies required to carry out the role is that of 'customer care', think of a situation that you have previously been in where you provided an exceptional level of customer service. Because the role that you are applying for is one of 'safety critical', try to think of any experience or qualifications you have where you have worked in this type of role. You may also consider attending a Health and Safety course in order to improve your knowledge in this area.

CHAPTER 2
THE ASSESSABLE COMPETENCIES

In this short chapter I will make reference to the competencies that you will be assessed against during every stage of the Traffic Officer selection process. I cannot emphasis enough how important these are. If you fail to match them during every stage of the process, then you will fail. Therefore, it is crucial that you have a thorough understanding of them, why they are important, and also be able to provide evidence of where you match each and every one of them.

To competencies that you will be assessed against during the HATO selection process include:

- Communicates well with others (Communicating and Marketing)

- Taking responsibility for, and pride in, the delivery of your own work (Leadership)

- Providing the best quality service to our customers (Customer service)

- Working with other teams, organisations and the public (Partnership Working and Stakeholder Management)

- Ensuring safety of yourself, colleagues and the public (Safety)

- Working under pressure to manage incidents and conflict (Incident Management)

In order to help you gain a full understanding of each assessable competency, I will now provide an explanation of what each one means, and how you can match it during the selection process.

COMMUNICATES WELL WITH OTHERS (COMMUNICATING AND MARKETING)

As you would expect Traffic Officer's need to be capable of communicating effectively, not only with members of the public, but also with other stakeholders and agencies such as the Police, Fire Service and Ambulance Service. After all, these are the people whom they will be working with day in, day out. It would be of little use if a Traffic Officer was incapable of communicating facts about an incident to the police in a calm and controlled manner, carefully making sure that he/she provided all of the relevant details pertaining to the incident. Therefore, the Highways Agency will want to see evidence of effective communication during the selection process.

What does this mean during the selection process? This means:

- Completing the application form accurately and correctly. Make sure you follow all instructions that are provided, not only on the application form, but also within the

recruitment guidance notes. Be sure to read these carefully before completing your application form. If you fail to follow instructions carefully, then you could fail.

- During the role play scenarios that form part of the assessment centre, make sure you deal with the role play actors in a calm manner. Never become aggressive, confrontational or panic. You must be in control at all times and communicate in a clear, concise and effective manner.

- During the interview you should speak in a clear and concise manner. When speaking to the interview panel look them in the eye, speak up and be clear in your responses.

TAKING RESPONSIBILITY FOR, AND PRIDE IN, THE DELIVERY OF YOUR OWN WORK (LEADERSHIP)

As with any uniformed service it is crucial that you take responsibility for performing to a high standard. You are acting as a role model for the Highways Agency and therefore you should be capable of setting a good example to other work colleagues, other road users and other services that you may work with. It is also imperative that you can carry out your work in a safe and competent manner. The UK's highways are a dangerous place to work. You must always have the safety of yourself, your work colleagues, your equipment and other road users at the forefront of your mind.

What does this mean during the selection process? This means:

- Complete the application form in a concise, accurate and neat manner. Take a pride in the appearance of your form. Make sure it is readable and that there are no spelling/grammar errors.

- Responding to 'situational' interview questions by providing examples of where you have demonstrated responsibility in a previous role.

PROVIDING THE BEST QUALITY SERVICE TO OUR CUSTOMERS (CUSTOMER SERVICE)

On many occasions during your career as a Traffic Officer you will be required to interact with other road users. These other road users are your customers. Road users pay taxes and it is these taxes that ultimately fund the Highways Agency. Therefore, it is only right and proper that the Highways Agency provides a high quality service to its customers.

At all times during your working career with the Highways Agency you should provide a high level of customer service.

What does this mean during the selection process? This means:

- Providing examples during the application form and the interview of where you have already demonstrated high quality customer care.

- Treating the role actor in a polite and considerate manner during the assessment centre taking care never to become confrontational or aggressive.

WORKING WITH OTHER TEAMS, ORGANISATIONS AND THE PUBLIC (PARTNERSHIP WORKING AND STAKEHOLDER MANAGEMENT)

Team work is an essential part of the Traffic Officers role. Just like the Police Force, Fire Service and Ambulance Service, the Highways Agency works with other organisations and stakeholders. The term 'stakeholder' essentially means any

other organisation or body that has a vested interest in the Highways Agency. Examples are:

- The Fire and Rescue Service

- The Police Force

- The Ambulance Service

- The AA/RAC and other roadside recovery organisations

- The environmental agency

- The Local Authority

Whilst working as a Traffic Officer you will come into regular contact with all of the above stakeholders.

What does this mean during the selection process? This means:

- Providing evidence of previous experience in relation to team working during your responses to the application form questions and the interview.

- Demonstrating an ability to work as part of a team during the assessment centre.

ENSURING SAFETY OF YOURSELF, COLLEAGUES AND THE PUBLIC (SAFETY)

Health and safety in any workplace is paramount. However, health and safety whilst working as a Traffic Officer is of even more importance. The reason for this is simply because you will be working in an environment that is fraught with danger. High speeding traffic, road traffic collisions (RTCs), chemical spills, fire and other such dangers will be a common occurrence during your career. This is the very reason why the Highways Agency makes this competency an assessable

area. Have the word 'safety' at the forefront of your mind when completing the application form and responding to the interview questions.

What does this mean during the selection process? This means:

- Providing evidence of previous experience in relation to safe working practices or working in a safety critical role.

- Demonstrating an ability to work safely during the assessment centre and also taking into account safety issue during the role play scenarios.

WORKING UNDER PRESSURE TO MANAGE INCIDENTS AND CONFLICT (INCIDENT MANAGEMENT)

As a Traffic Officer you will be required to work under pressure. The pressure will come from having to deal with members of the public who are panicking following an incident, being first on the scene of a Road Traffic Collision that involves many casualties, dealing with fatalities, cordoning off a scene or incident and also communicating important messages to your control centre. The ability to remain calm and focused during a difficult incident is vital. Therefore, the Highways Agency assessment team will want to see evidence of your ability to achieve this during the selection process.

What does this mean during the selection process? This means:

- Providing evidence of previous experience in relation to working under pressure in a previous role whilst completing the application form and responding to interview questions.

- Demonstrating an ability to work under pressure during the role play scenarios.

It is extremely important that you focus on the above assessable competencies whilst you are progressing through the selection process. You must try to demonstrate evidence of where you can match each and everyone one of them during the different part of the process. I will make continued reference to them as we progress through the book.

CHAPTER 3
THE SELECTION PROCESS

A BRIEF INTRODUCTION TO THE HATO SELECTION PROCESS

The Highways Agency is no different to any modern day professional organisation in the fact that they want to ensure they carry out a transparent and fair recruitment process. Everyone who applies to become a Traffic Officer will go through the same selection process.

To begin with you will need to ensure that you are sure this is the job for you. Whilst the HATO job is a brilliant one to have, you need to ensure that it is for you. Read the job description contained within this guide and also on the Highways Agencies website. Be sure that you have the potential to carry out the job safely and effectively. Once you are satisfied that this job is for you, you will need to see when the next recruitment campaign is running. This can be done by visiting the following website:

http://www.highways.gov.uk

If the Highways Agency are not recruiting in your area do not worry, they will be at some point in the future. You can sign up to e-mail alerts which will keep you up to date and tell you when the next recruitment drive in your regional area is taking place. In the meantime, and in between recruitment drives, you can start to prepare for the HATO selection process. The first part of the selection process requires you to complete a comprehensive application form and also a diversity questionnaire. Whilst the diversity questionnaire is not compulsory I do recommend that you take the time to complete it as it will allow the Highways Agency to monitor their recruitment progress.

Once you have completed the application form the Highways Agency will thoroughly check it to see whether you meet the minimum eligibility requirements. It is important that you send off the application well in time to beat the closing date as late applications are not considered. I also advise that when returning your application form you send it recorded or special delivery, unless of course you are required to submit the form online. Unfortunately some items can go missing in the post, so this extra precaution of sending it recorded delivery will guarantee your application gets received. If you are submitting your application form online then again it is important that you send it in plenty of time prior to the closing date. The Highways Agency has many applications to sift through and the earlier your submission is received the better.

If you are successful during the initial application form stage then you will be invited to attend a comprehensive assessment centre. During the assessment centre you will be tested by a variety of different means including role

play and interviews. Many organisations use role play as a means of assessing your likely behaviour in a specific work related scenario. If you successfully pass the assessment centre then you may receive an offer of appointment if other checks into you nationality, qualifications, health and other important matters are satisfactory.

If it is not possible to immediately put you into a post due to insufficient vacancies in your chosen location(s) then you could be placed on a waiting list for a set period of time. As soon as a vacancy becomes available then you will be offered it.

CHAPTER 4
THE APPLICATION FORM

HOW TO COMPLETE THE APPLICATION FORM

Once you have received your application form/pack the first step is to go through it and read it thoroughly. This will allow you to understand more about the role that you are applying for and also to read the instructions that relate to how the form should be completed. It is essential that you take the time to read the guidance notes carefully before completing the form.

The competition is fierce so you need to ensure you complete the form both correctly and accurately.

The guidance notes
As mentioned above, before you complete the application form it is important that you read the guidance notes, especially the section that relates to your skills and abilities for the job. This section is very important and carries the

 how2become

biggest weight in terms of points available. If you fail to get this part right then your form will not make it through the sift stage.

Part of the guidance notes makes reference to sections 16 and 17 and it even tells you how important these sections are! The Highways Agency want to know about you, your life experiences, qualifications, relevant qualifications, skills and abilities so it is essential that you provide them with what they are looking for. It recommends against each competency/essential requirement that you give examples of a past experience that best illustrate the qualities they are looking for.

- If qualifications/experience forms part of the essential criteria then you must tell them **how** you match the requirements, more on this later.

- You must give one recent example for each competency/ essential requirement.

- You should be precise about what you did and the part you played in the activities you describe. It is no good telling them what you *would* do in this type of situation, but rather you must give a specific example of where you *have* already met the competency/requirement.

A simple, yet effective way to explain what they are after here is as follows. Take a look at the following competency:

COMPETENCY AREA ASSESSED:
Working with other teams, organisations and the public

Sample response – 'poor'
"If I was to work with other people then I believe I would have the right skills to do the job correctly and professionally.

I would always make sure I performed to a high standard and would work hard to get on well with other people".

The above example response is poor because it is 'generic'. Apart from being grammatically incorrect, the person talks about what they would do if they worked with other people as opposed to providing evidence of where they have worked with other people.

Now take a look at the following 'good' response:

Sample response – 'good'
"I recently volunteered to work with a new member our team at work. The task required us both to successfully complete a stock take of the entire warehouse within a short time frame. Initially I showed the new team member how to stock take in a professional manner in accordance with company guidelines. Once I had achieved this we both then set about methodically working through each aisle, stocktaking as we went along. Periodically we would stop to ensure that the task was being done correctly. We supported each other during the task and made sure that we kept a watchful eye on the time and the progress that we were making. At the end of the specified timeframe we had completed the stock take and were able to provide accurate figures to our line manager".

The above response, whilst only 135 words in length, is effective. It conforms to the S.T.A.R principle of answering competency based questions and is also relatively easy to follow, concise and grammatically correct.

THE S.T.A.R PRINCIPLE EXPLAINED

Specific – make sure your responses to each competency being assessed are specific. Provide an actual recent

example of where you have met the competency. You will get marked down for being too generic. Don't say what you *'would do'* but rather say what you *'have done'*.

Task – briefly describe the task that you were required to carry out. In the above sample response the person has described the task in one sentence as follows:

"The task required us both to successfully complete a complete stock take of the entire warehouse within a short timeframe."

This sentence sets the scene and tells the person who is reading the response exactly what was required as part of your task. It is important that all of your responses follow a logical sequence of events and the STAR method allows you to do just that.

Action – during this part of your response you will detail what action you took. Remember that your response needs to be specific so you will need to state what you did, rather than what you would do in such a situation. An example of a detailed action response is as follows:

"Initially I showed the new team member how to stock take in a professional manner in accordance with company guidelines. Once I had achieved this we both then set about methodically working through each aisle, stocktaking as we went along. Periodically we would stop to ensure that the task was being done correctly."

Result – finally, at the end of your response you need to explain what the outcome was to your actions. It is always a good idea to end on a positive note. If you achieved the task successfully then you should state this. You will see from the example provided previously that the result was positive:

"At the end of the specified timeframe we had completed the stock take and were able to provide accurate figures to our line manager".

WORD COUNT

Many employers, when requiring competency based responses to questions will require a set 'word count' that cannot be exceeded. The reason for the word count is twofold. Firstly the employer cannot spend hours working through your responses. They receive many hundreds of applications per recruitment campaign so they need to allocate a set amount of time to each stage of the selection process. Secondly, you should be able to demonstrate your ability to meet the competencies being assessed in a few words. If you read what is required and have the ability to construct concise, yet relevant responses then your chances of success will increase.

In the case of the Highways Agency Traffic Officer application form the word count, per response to the competency assessment, is usually around the 200 word mark. Read the application form carefully and make sure you stick to the maximum number of words. The most effective way to achieve this is to create your response in Microsoft Word. By selecting 'tools' and then 'word count' you will be able to quickly assess how many words your response is.

Don't go over the maximum number of words but also do not go too far under either!

SAMPLE RESPONSES TO THE COMPETENCY BASED ASSESSMENT

On the HATO application form you will be required to

answer questions that relate to the competencies that are being assessed. This is an extremely important part of the application form so it is important that you take the time to get it right.

The first step in ensuring you get this part right is to download the 'role description' for the job that you are applying for. This can be achieved by visiting the Highways Agency website at:

http://www.highways.gov.uk

Once you have downloaded a copy of the job description you must read it fully and in particular focus on the key core competencies that are required to carry out the job competently.

Examples of the areas that may be assessed include:

• Communicating and marketing

• Leadership and taking responsibility

• Customer service

• Working with others

• Safety

• Working under pressure

You will quickly identify that all of the above competencies are key skills required to perform the role of a Traffic Officer competently.

As a Traffic Officer you are required to **work with others**. Not only with colleagues whilst on patrol but also working with other agencies such as the Police, Fire Service, Transport Agencies and other similar organisations. You will also be required to work closely with your control centre, albeit on a more 'verbal communication' basis than face to face.

The Highways Agency provides a brilliant service to the road users whom it serves. Therefore you will need to have good **customer service skills** and these will be assessed at each stage of the selection process.

Communicating obviously plays an important part of your role. On a daily basis you will need to speak to and liaise with other road users and services. Therefore your communication skills and powers of influence will need to be good.

Safety is absolutely paramount. Not only will you be driving and operating on busy roads and networks, you will also be responsible for the safety of other road users, your colleagues and your equipment.

As a Traffic Officer you will be required to **take responsibility** and make important decisions on a daily basis, whilst **working under pressure**. This takes skill. Imagine being the first person to arrive on the scene of a Road Traffic Collision. There is chaos and the emergency services are 15 minutes away. What do you do and how do you prioritise each task? Yes you will receive comprehensive and professional training but even so, you will still need to solve difficult problems whilst under pressure.

So, you can begin to understand the importance of the competencies being assessed and how you must take the time to demonstrate you have the skills and experience to meet them. If you can provide evidence of where you have met the competencies being assessed then you may have the potential to become a Traffic Officer.

Over the next few pages I have provided a small number of examples of how I would match the assessable criteria whilst completing the application form. Read the examples carefully before using the blank templates to create your

own responses based on your own skills and experiences. You will notice that I have deliberately left out two assessable areas, that of 'safety' and 'taking responsibility'. Once you have read the sample responses provided, take the time to create your own individual responses to each assessable area.

SAMPLE RESPONSES TO THE COMPETENCY BASED ASSESSMENT

Let us now take a look at a sample fictitious response to the first competency being assessed – working with others:

Working with others

"I recently volunteered to work with a new member our team at work. The task required us both to successfully complete a stock take of the entire warehouse within a short timeframe. The reason why I volunteered for the task is because I am a conscientious person who enjoys working with other people, and carrying out tasks to a high standard.

Initially I showed the new team member how to stock take in a professional manner in accordance with company guidelines. He had never carried out this type of work before and I wanted to ensure he was both comfortable with the task and that he was doing it correctly. Once I had achieved this we both then set about methodically working through each aisle, stocktaking as we went along. Periodically we would stop to ensure that the task was being done correctly. At the end of the specified timeframe we had completed the stock take and were able to provide accurate figures to our line manager.

Whilst working as a team member I always concentrate on effective communication, focusing on the task in hand and providing support to team members who require assistance."

Word count 196

You will see that the above sample response, whilst under the maximum word count of 200, follows the STAR principle.

Now use the template that follows to create your own unique response to this assessable area.

TEMPLATE - Working with others

SAMPLE RESPONSES TO THE COMPETENCY BASED ASSESSMENT

Customer service

"Whilst working as a sales representative for my current employer, I received a telephone call from an unhappy customer. It was my task to resolve the situation to his satisfaction whilst operating in accordance with company guidelines. I started out by listening to his concerns and taking detailed notes about his complaint. I informed him that I fully understood his concerns and I reassured him that I would do everything possible to help him and resolve the issue. I immediately dispatched another order whilst on the phone to him, making sure that the order would be delivered that same day. I also told him that I would call him later that day to make sure he was happy with the new order.

Later that day, I telephoned the gentleman to check everything was to his satisfaction. The sound in his voice was very rewarding and I realised that with just a little help I had made such a difference to his day, making him feel like a valued customer.

The result of the situation was that an initially unhappy customer was now happy with the service he had received and the company had maintained its positive image."

Word count 197

You will see that the above sample response once again follows the STAR principle and also turns a negative situation into a positive one. The person is totally focused on the customer and makes sure the situation ends on a positive note. Finally, remember to be specific.

TEMPLATE - Customer Service

SAMPLE RESPONSES TO THE COMPETENCY BASED ASSESSMENT

Communicating

"Whilst working as a mechanic in my current job I was faced with a situation where a customer, following a routine service, did not want to have an important piece of safety critical work carried out on her car. My task was to explain to her the dangers that she faced by not having the work carried out, and influence her to proceed with the work.

I started out by explaining in simple terms the reason for the fault and the fact that she had been driving around with this dangerous problem for some time. I also explained the consequences of not having the work carried out as a matter of urgency and reassured her that the problem was genuine.

After careful communication and a detailed explanation of the problem and the dangers she faced, she finally agreed to have the work carried out there and then. I fully understood how she must have been feeling and was sensitive in my communication approach.

The result was that the lady would now have a safe car to drive and therefore herself and her family would not be exposed to any unnecessary dangers."

Word count 191

You will see that the above sample response once again follows the STAR principle and also covers two important aspects – communicating and influencing. Communication skills are very important to your role as a Traffic Officer so make sure you provide a suitable response that demonstrates your ability to both communicate effectively and use reasoned influencing skills.

TEMPLATE - Communicating

SAMPLE RESPONSES TO THE COMPETENCY BASED ASSESSMENT

Working under pressure

"In my current role as customer service manager, I am required to work under pressure on a daily basis. Recently, I was presented with a situation where two members of staff had gone sick leaving me with only two other staff members to manage the shop during a busy Saturday.

During the morning, we were due to take a stock delivery, which meant that I had to perform many tasks within a short period of time. In addition to the stock delivery duties I dealt with two customer complaints, carried out an inventory of all the stock, served customers whilst others took their break and, also, dealt with a fire alarm actuation. I ensured that the level of service delivery was high throughout this period of pressurised working. I was able to complete each task on time and to a high standard. The result, at the end of the working day, was that each task was carried out successfully and to a very high standard.

I am often required to perform under pressure and thrive in such conditions. I always adapt well to situations like these and ensure that I still maintain a high level of professionalism at all times."

Word count 200

Once again, the above sample response follows the STAR principle and also covers a specific example of where the candidate had to work under pressure. As a Traffic Officer you will be required to work under pressurised circumstances on a daily basis so make sure you provide an example that demonstrates you can carry out a number of tasks within a specified timeframe.

TEMPLATE - Working under pressure

FINAL TIPS FOR INCREASING YOUR CHANCES OF SUCCESS

- Make sure you use the STAR method when creating your responses.

- Try to incorporate keywords and phrases that encompass the STAR principle.

  For example:

  "The task I was required to perform included…"

  "I action I took involved…"

  "The result, following my actions was…"

- Try to include a positive outcome to your actions.

- Make sure you are specific. Provide an actual situation that you were involved in.

- Read the job description and person specification before completing your form and ensure you can meet the minimum eligibility requirements.

- Check your grammar, punctuation and spelling carefully before you submit your application.

- Make a copy of your application before you submit it. You will need to refer back to this prior to your interview.

CHAPTER 5
ROLE PLAYS

THE ROLE PLAY EXERCISES

Many employers, including the Highways Agency, now use Role Play as a means of assessing a candidates potential to meet the requirements of a specific role. During the Traffic Officer assessment you will be required to perform a number of different role plays. Whilst role play scenarios are somewhat difficult to predict in terms of style and the actual scenario you will be required to undertake, there are a number of important things you can do in order to prepare for them.

The exact types of simulation will vary between each assessment centre but the core behaviours that you are required to demonstrate are the generally the same throughout.

Providing you pay attention to what is required and learn

to incorporate the core assessable behaviours into each simulation, you will greatly increase your chances of success. Some of the more common types of simulation that are used at assessment centres are as follows:

• Dealing with a complaint

• Giving constructive criticism

• Taking criticism

• Dealing with a request for help

• Calming somebody down

• Listening with a purpose

Whilst these are quite vague in terms of their description, you can begin to feel the type of simulation you will be up against during the Traffic Officer assessment. The most effective way to prepare for the role play exercises is to keep an open mind about the type of simulation you will come across.

During each of the simulations you will be given a non work related based role that you will assume whilst in the assessment room. The Highways Agency recruitment staff want to see that you have the potential to deal with specific situations in an effective manner and you will find that the simulations you are asked to deal with are similar to those that a Traffic Officer may come across in his or her role. The Highways Agency expect you to be yourself and deal with the simulations in the same way you would deal with similar situations you meet in everyday life. However, there are a number of things that you can do to improve your chances of success on the day, which we will cover on the following pages. Read each of the following areas carefully and try to understand how each of them can fit into the role of a Traffic Officer.

KEY AREA 1 - NON-VERBAL LISTENING SKILLS

How you show that you are listening

This is your ability to demonstrate, through your body language, facial expressions and general demeanour that you can effectively listen to what other people are saying. In all of the Role Play simulations you will be required to listen effectively to what people are saying and demonstrate that you are doing this through a number of ways, which are indicated as follows:

How to listen effectively during the role play scenarios

1. Face the role actor and maintain eye contact but avoid any confrontational stares or aggressive facial expressions.

2. Use simple body language to show the speaker that you are listening to them. Do not fold your arms or puff your chest out as this will portray a confrontational stance.

3. Keep an open mind at all times.

4. Listen to the words and try to picture what the speaker is saying.

5. Don't interrupt and don't impose your "solutions". You should only interrupt if the role actor becomes verbally abusive, aggressive or uses inappropriate language. If they do, remain calm and ask them politely to refrain from using that type of language. It is important to be assertive when the need arises, however, being assertive does not mean being aggressive.

6. Wait for the speaker to pause before asking clarifying questions.

7. Ask questions only to ensure understanding of something that has been said (avoiding questions that disrupt the speaker's train of thought).

8. Try to feel what the speaker is feeling.

9. Give the speaker regular feedback, e.g. summarise, reflect feelings, or simply say "uh huh".

10. Pay attention to what isn't said - to feelings, facial expressions, gestures, posture and other non-verbal cues.

KEY AREA 2 - SUSPENDING JUDGEMENT

How and when to make judgements and decisions

This is all about the timing of your decisions or judgements. How far do you let something go or carry on for before making your judgement or making a decision? One of the assessable competencies is that of 'leadership' and 'taking responsibility'. This effectively means that you will be required to make decisions based on facts and information that is presented before you.

You will need to listen to the information that you are receiving from the role actor and make a decision about when to interact. For example, if the role play scenario involved having to deal with an injured casualty, then you would need to make your judgement very quickly. One of the most important elements of a Traffic Officers role is the need to communicate accurate and correct information that relates to incidents on the roads. Depending on the scenario that you are presented with during the role plays, try to gather all of the relevant facts first before making any decisions and always remember to stay calm and in control.

KEY AREA 3 – ASSERTION

Making your case without being aggressive or yielding
This is quite a difficult 'skill' to master but one that is important if you are to pass the Traffic Officer assessment. Try to think of how you would react as a Traffic Officer if a frustrated road user started to blame you for the traffic congestion after you had stopped to help them during a break down. Would you argue with them and make the situation worse? Or would you deal with the situation in a calm but effective manner, with the emphasis on avoiding making the situation worse by using effective defusing skills?

With any simulation that requires the core behaviour of assertion, you must learn to be assertive and firm without coming across as aggressive. This may mean that you need to raise your voice above the person who is shouting at you, but make sure you don't shout aggressively or in a yielding manner. Stay very calm and make sure your body language shows this. Any sign of aggression on your part will not gain you any points.

Take a look at the following two examples of how a Traffic Officer might defuse the situation explained in the previous paragraph.

Poor way of dealing with the situation
"Now you listen to me Sir and listen carefully. If you don't stop shouting and being aggressive then I am going to call the Police, and you don't want me to do that I can assure you!"

Good way of dealing with the situation
"Sir, I fully appreciate how you must be feeling right now but I would respectfully ask that you stay calm. I have pulled over

to assist you and to also make sure you and your family are safe whilst we wait for breakdown recovery to arrive."

You will notice that the second example of how to deal with the situation is far more effective and is aimed at explaining how the Traffic Officer is trying to help the individual concerned. This can be done in a calm yet assertive manner.

KEY AREA 4 - EXPLORING AND CLARIFYING

How you establish information
During your role play assessment you will need to ask questions in order to find out what has happened in a situation. For example, if somebody has made a complaint about a specific situation you will need to ask them questions.

Probing questions such as *"Where did that happen?"*, *"What time did the incident occur?"*, *"Was anybody else involved?"*, *"Who was involved?"* will all give you information that was probably not initially forthcoming. Whatever the simulation you are confronted with, ask probing questions to gather the information you need in order to make effective judgements and decisions.

KEY AREA 5 - RESPECT FOR DIVERSITY

How you demonstrate respect for all people
Respect for everybody within society and the workplace is very important. Respect for a person's religious beliefs, sexual orientation, race, colour, age etc, is fundamental to the Traffic Officers role. How would you react in a role play if you were confronted by a work colleague who was gay? Would you treat them any differently because they were gay? Hopefully you wouldn't. If you do not have respect for diversity then you should not be applying for the role of a

Traffic Officer. During all of the simulations remember to have total respect for diversity and treat everybody fairly and appropriately based on their own individual needs.

KEY AREA 6 – CUSTOMER SERVICE

How you treat people in the workplace

As you are now fully aware, customer service is one of the assessable areas. The Highways Agency is focused on providing an exceptional level of customer service. During the role play scenarios you will be required to demonstrate an ability to provide an excellent level of customer care. This will be assessed in how you speak, how you react, and also in the decisions you make during each scenario.

TIPS FOR PASSING THE TRAFFIC OFFICER ROLE PLAY EXERCISES

- Listen carefully to what is being said both during the assessment centre brief and during each role play simulation.

- Practice demonstrating the assessable competencies prior to attending the assessment centre and role plays.

- Practice non-verbal listening skills in front of the mirror. You should be able to tell how effective your body language and facial expressions are by just looking in the mirror.

- Think about how you would react in a confrontational situation. You need to make sure you can stay calm under pressure and have the ability to defuse any situation. If you feel a situation getting out of hand, don't panic but rather stay calm.

On the following pages I have provided you with a number of sample role play exercises and responses. Please note that these are only examples and will NOT be the exact scenarios you will face on the day but instead are provided as a practice resource during your preparation.

SAMPLE ROLE PLAY EXERCISE 1

SCENARIO You are the Customer Service Manager at a fictitious retail centre. A member of your staff approaches you and tells you that another member of staff has been making racist comments about her. She would like to make a complaint.

HOW TO PREPARE

To begin with you need to read the briefing sheet carefully or listen to the brief from the recruitment staff. What does it/ they tell you about the scenario and are there any clues that dictate how you should respond to the situation? Remember to think about the key areas described previously in this section and how you can relate them to the scenario. In this instance you will certainly need to demonstrate 'non-verbal listening' skills. This can be achieved by utilising effective body language and facial expressions. The person has clearly had a terrible experience and you need to reflect this in your response.

With a situation such as a complaint you must be competent in taking down the relevant information about the situation. Remember to show respect for diversity at all times.

Once you have listened to what the person has to say, you will need to ask probing questions, exploring and clarifying what has happened before making a judgement. Make sure you resolve the situation and check with the person that they

are happy with your proposed plan of action.

There now follows a sample response to help you prepare.

SAMPLE RESPONSE TO ROLE PLAY EXERCISE 1

"Hello madam, thank you for coming to see me today. I understand you've had a bad experience? Please can you tell me exactly what happened?"

LISTEN TO WHAT IS BEING SAID AND SHOW THAT YOU ARE LISTENING THROUGH EFFECTIVE LISTENING SKILLS, BOTH VERBAL AND NONVERBAL

"That must have been terrible for you, are you okay for me to ask you some questions about the situation? If at anytime you feel uncomfortable please stop me and we will take a break."

TAKE NOTE

'What did the person say to you?'

'When and where did this happen?'

'How did that make you feel?'

'Have they said anything like this to you before?'

'Are you aware of anybody else receiving the same treatment?'

"Thank you for the information you have provided me with today. I can assure you that this kind of behaviour will not be tolerated and a full investigation will be carried out. In the meantime is there anything I can do to make your working day easier?

"In order to resolve this situation I propose to take the following action..."

"I promise you that I will be in touch soon to let you know how things are progressing. Please don't hesitate in coming to see me if anything else happens. Are you satisfied with my proposal?"

FURTHER ADVICE - SAMPLE ROLE PLAY EXERCISE 1

When dealing with any complaint of this nature you must demonstrate empathy and understanding for the other person's situation. Try to put yourself in their shoes, how would you feel if it was you on the receiving end of this kind of treatment?

Always remember the following key areas that will help you to successfully pass any role play scenario:

- Have respect for diversity at all times.

- Explore and clarify. This means asking questions and then checking for understanding.

- Where possible, suspend judgement before making any decisions.

- Show understanding and empathy if the situation requires it.

- Demonstrate assertion when required but never become aggressive or confrontational.

- Demonstrate non-verbal and verbal listening skills.

- Always challenge inappropriate, aggressive or abusive language quickly but in a clam manner.

Every role play simulation or exercise must be based upon its own merits and your judgement on how you deal with the situation should be based upon the situation itself. Try not to

get too entrenched in the type of assessment you will be up against, but instead improve your skills in the above areas.

SAMPLE ROLE PLAY EXERCISE 2

Whilst working in a shop you are approached by a customer who is not happy with the level of service she has received.

HOW TO PREPARE

During the role play assessment you may encounter a simulation that involves an angry, confrontational person. The scenario itself is irrelevant; the way you deal with it is the main priority and is what you will be assessed against. You may walk into the role-play room and find a person will immediately start raising their voice at you, so be prepared for such an event and don't get caught out. To begin with you need to remain calm and not be frightened by the experience.

Your assertion in such scenarios is an area that will be assessed and you need to stand your ground providing the situation dictates. As a Traffic Officer you will need to defuse potentially confrontational situations, and this type of scenario will test your ability to do just that. I have now provided you with some useful tips and advice on how to deal with confrontational situations like this one.

USEFUL TIPS FOR DEALING WITH ROLE PLAY EXERCISE 2

- Be prepared for a confrontational response as soon as you enter the room. It is essential that you remain calm and do not react to the aggression.

- Show good positive body language and do not fight fire with fire.

- Listen to what is being said.

- Use effective judgement about when to intervene but do not use any form of body contact such as holding or touching.

- Defuse the situation in a calm manner. Do not rise to the bait by becoming aggressive yourself. This will lose you marks and you could end up failing as a result.

- Use open body language.

- NEVER argue with the person.

- Be assertive in your response but ensure you are calm at all times.

- Try to get the person to calm down.

- If a chair is available then ask them to sit down.

- Adopt non-threatening, but not submissive body language. Keep a clear, calm tone of voice.

- If you feel that the situation is getting worse then do not panic. You will score higher marks if you just stay calm.

- Use phrases such as 'please calm down', 'let me try and help you' and 'let's work together to try and resolve this situation'.

SAMPLE ROLE PLAY SCENARIO 3

ABOUT YOU
You are the Customer Service Manager at a fictitious retail centre. You are responsible for:

- Investigating complaints from both customers and staff.

- Dealing with any complaints of bullying or harassment.

- Ensuring the highest of standards are always maintained.

- Dealing with under performing employees and recommending an appropriate course of action.

The retail centre does not tolerate any form of bullying, harassment or discrimination and anyone found to be in contravention of these rules will face disciplinary procedures.

YOUR BRIEF
You are approached by a customer who is not happy with the level of service he has received. He wants to discuss this with you. The company has strict guidelines relating to high levels of customer service. It is your responsibility to speak to the customer and resolve their complaint.

SAMPLE RESPONSE TO ROLE PLAY EXERCISE 3

It is important that you remain calm when dealing with angry or confrontational people. If you enter the role play scenario and the actor is being confrontational or slightly aggressive then remain calm and do not get drawn in to an argument.

"Hello Sir, I am the Customer Service Manager and I am here to help you. Please can you explain what the problem is?"

Listen carefully to what is being said by demonstrating non-verbal listening skills. This might mean nodding your head whilst the role actor is speaking.

Ask questions in order to gather the evidence you need in order to resolve the situation.

"From what you are saying I understand that you don't feel happy with the service you have received. Can I just ask you a few questions about what has happened so that I can gain a fuller picture of the scenario? This will allow me to deal with your complaint in a fast and efficient manner."

You should sympathise with the person's situation and apologise if appropriate.

"I am very sorry that you have received this level of service and I fully sympathise with your predicament. I will do all that I can to resolve it for you."

Try to come up with a plan of action that resolves the situation for the person aggrieved.

"Now that I have gathered all of the facts, I can now deal with your complaint effectively. This is what I plan to do..."

Check with the person to see if they are happy with your proposed plan of action.

"Can I just check sir to make sure you are happy with my proposed plan of action?"

CHAPTER 6
THE TRAFFIC OFFICER INTERVIEW

HOW TO PASS THE TRAFFIC OFFICER INTERVIEW

During this section of the guide I will provide you with some useful tips on how to prepare for the Traffic Officer interview. The Traffic Officer Interview does not have to be a daunting process, providing that is you prepare effectively. Yes, any interview can be a nerve-wracking experience, but if you prepare in the right areas this will give the confidence you need to pass with flying colours. Within this section of the guide I have provided you with a number of sample questions that you may get asked during your Interview. The panel will normally consist of at least one senior member of the Highways Agency and a representative from the Human Resources department. The Human Resources representative is present to ensure that the interview is carried out fairly and in conjunction with company policy and guidelines. Every candidate will be asked the same

 how2become

questions to ensure consistency and fairness.

HOW TO PREPARE EFFECTIVELY

During your preparation for the interview I would recommend that you concentrate on the following three key areas:

- Interview technique;

- Research;

- Responding to the interview questions.

Each of the above areas is equally important. I will now go into each one of them in detail:

INTERVIEW TECHNIQUE

Interview technique covers a number of different areas. The majority of candidates will pay it little, if any attention at all. Interview technique basically involves the following key areas:

Creating the right impression
When you walk into the interview room you should stand up tall, smile and be polite and courteous to the panel. Do not sit down in the interview chair until invited to do so.

Being presentable
During my time as an interviewer for a number of different jobs I have been amazed at the number of people who turn up inappropriately dressed. I have seen people turn up for interviews in jeans, t shirts and trainers! I strongly advise that you take the time to look smart and presentable. Remember you are applying to join an organisation that requires you to wear a uniform. If you dress smart and formal for the interview,

then you are far more likely to wear your uniform with pride. Presentation effectively means how I intend to dress for the interview, and also how I intend to come across. I want the interview panel to see me as a professional, motivated, conscientious and caring person who is taking the interview very seriously.

Some interviews, especially those in the public sector, do not require you to dress formally. For some bizarre reason, some senior managers believe that a person should not be assessed on how they present themselves at interview. Personally, I disagree with this approach. Whilst I agree there is no need to go out and buy an expensive suit or a new pair of shoes, I do believe that a potential employee should make an effort in their appearance. After all, they are going to be a role model for the service.

For any job interview I will make sure that my suit is cleaned and pressed, my shoes are polished, and my personal hygiene is up to standard. This means simple things such as taking a shower, shaving, having a haircut and general grooming. I will always avoid brightly coloured clothes and generally go for a conservative approach such a dark blue, black or grey suit. If I do decide to wear any brighter, more vibrant colours, then this will be in form of a tie. I would strongly advise that you avoid brightly coloured socks or ties with cartoon characters on them!

A good applicant
A good applicant is someone who has taken the time to prepare. They have researched both the organisation they are applying to join and also the role that they are being interviewed for. They may not know every detail about the organisation and the role but it will be clear that they have made an effort to find out important facts and information.

They will be well presented at the interview and they will be confident, but not overconfident. As soon as they walk into the interview room they will be polite and courteous and they will sit down in the interview chair only when invited to do so. Throughout the interview they will sit upright in the chair and communicate in a positive manner. If they do not know the answer to a question they will say so and they won't try to waffle. At the end of the interview they will ask positive questions about the job or the organisation before shaking hands and leaving.

A poor applicant

A poor applicant could be any combination of the following. They will be late for the interview or even forget to turn up at all. They will have made little effort to dress smartly and they will have carried out little or no preparation. When asked questions about the role they will have little or no knowledge. Throughout the interview they will appear to be unenthusiastic about the whole process and will look as if they want the interview to be over as soon as possible. Whilst sat in the interview chair they will slouch and fidget. At the end of the interview they will try to ask clever questions that are intended to impress the panel.

Improving interview technique

How you present yourself during the interview is important. Whilst assessing candidates for interviews I will not only assess their responses to the interview questions but I will also pay attention to the way they present themselves. A candidate could give excellent responses to the interview questions but if they present themselves in a negative manner, then this can lose them marks.

Take a look at the following diagrams, which indicate both poor technique and good technique.

POOR INTERVIEW TECHNIQUE

His elbow is resting on the corner of the chair, which indicates an over-confident attitude.

The candidate's legs are crossed and his feet are not resting on the floor. This displays a relaxed and casual manner.

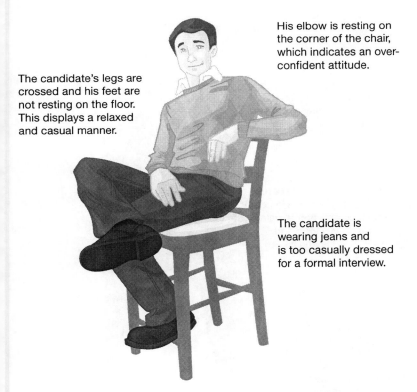

The candidate is wearing jeans and is too casually dressed for a formal interview.

The candidate appears to be too relaxed and casual for an interview.

GOOD INTERVIEW TECHNIQUE

The candidate is smiling and he portrays a confident, but not over-confident manner.

The candidate is dressed wearing a smart suit. It is clear that he has made an effort in his presentation.

His hands are in a stable position, which will prevent him from fidgeting. He could also place his hands palms facing downwards and resting on his knees.

He is sitting upright in the interview chair with his feet resting on the floor. He is not slouching and he portrays himself in a positive manner.

In the build up to your interview practise a few mock interviews. Get a friend of relative to sit you down and ask you all of the questions that are contained within this section of the guide. Look to improve your interview technique as well as working on your responses to the interview questions.

Effective communication

Effective communication is all about how you speak to the interview panel, and also how you listen to what they have to say.

When responding to the interview questions you should speak clearly and concisely, avoiding all forms of waffle, slang or hesitations such as 'erm'. Look at each interview panel member when answering each question. Even though an interview question will be asked by one member of the panel at a time, you should always respond to the entire panel collectively. Look them in the eyes when speaking to them but never 'stare' them out. This will only portray you in an aggressive or confrontational manner.

If you are unsure about a response to an interview question then just be honest. Consider saying something along the lines of:

"I'm sorry I do not know the answer to that question. I will look the answer up as soon as I get back home and contact you to let you know the answer."

If they accept this response, make sure you do research the response and contact them to let them know.

When the interview panel are speaking to me, or if they are asking me a question, I will always demonstrate good listening skills. This means that I will use facial expressions to show that I am taking onboard what they are saying and I will also nod to show them that I understand the question(s).

Body language and posture

Whilst sat in the interview I will always make a conscious effort to sit upright and not slouch in the chair. I personally like to use my hands to emphasise points when responding to the questions but I will be careful not to overdo it. Even if the interview is going great and you are building up a good rapport with the panel, don't let your standards drop. Always maintain good body language and posture for the duration of the interview.

Final questions

Before I attend the interview I will always think of two questions to ask the panel at the end. However, don't be trapped in the thinking that you must ask questions. It is acceptable to say:

"Thank you but I don't have any questions. I have already carried out lots of research and you have answered some of my questions during the interview."

Some people believe that you must ask three, four or even five questions at the end of the interview – this is total nonsense. Remember that the interview panel will have other people to interview and they will also need time to discuss your performance.

If you do decide to ask questions then make sure they are relevant. Here's a couple of examples:

"I've been studying the Highways Agency website for some time now and have noticed that customer care is a high priority. Do you get many people using the customer care centre on the website?"

This type of question will show the panel that you have carried out your research and also that 'customer care' is high on your agenda.

"After researching the role of a Traffic Officer, I understand that they have to carry out 'rolling road blocks' to slow down the traffic in emergencies. How do Traffic Officers train for this type or work?"

This type of question demonstrates that you have researched the role of a Traffic Officer and also that you have a keen interest in their training.

A final parting statement

Once the interview has finished and you have asked your questions, you may wish to finish off with a final statement. Your final statement should say something about your desire and passion for becoming a Traffic Officer. The following is a good example of a final statement:

"I would like to say thank you for giving me the opportunity to be interviewed for the post today. Over the last few months I have been working hard to learn about the role of a Traffic Officer and also about the Highways Agency. If I am successful then I promise you that I will work hard to pass the tests and exams and I will be a loyal and professional employee of your team. Thank you."

RESEARCH

As you can imagine, in the build up to the interview you will need to carry out plenty of research. Research that is, in relation to the role of a Traffic Officer and also the Highways Agency. Here is a list of the more important areas I recommend that you study:

- The job description and person specification for the role that you are applying for. These are usually available through the website www.highways.gov.uk.

- Your application form and the responses that you provided.

- The website of the Highways Agency. What is their customer service or what is their customer promise? Do they have a mission statement? What services do they provide? What is the geographical area for the role that you are applying for? How many people work for the Highways Agency? Who is the person in charge? Where do they operate out of? What are the key roads?

- The type and duration of training that you will undergo once you have successfully passed selection.

Responding to the interview questions

If I were preparing for the Traffic Officer interview right now, I would take each area of the role individually and prepare a detailed response setting out where I meet the requirements of it.

Your response to each question that relates to the role of a Traffic Officer must be 'specific' in nature. This means that you need to provide an example of where you have already demonstrated the skills that are required under the job description or person specification in a previous role or situation. Do not fall into the trap of providing a 'generic' response that details what you 'would do' if the situation arose. Try to structure your responses in a logical and concise manner. The way to achieve this is to use the '**STAR**' method of interview question response construction:

SITUATION

Start off your response to the interview question by explaining what the 'situation' was and who was involved.

TASK

Once you have detailed the situation, explain what the 'task' was, or what needed to be done.

ACTION

Now explain what 'action' you took, and what action others took. Also explain why you took this particular course of action.

RESULT

Explain what the outcome or result was following your actions and those of others. Try to demonstrate in your response that the result was positive because of the action you took.

Finally, explain to the panel what you would do differently if the same situation arose again. It is good to be reflective at the end of your responses. This demonstrates a level of maturity and it will also show the panel that you are willing to learn from every experience.

The different types of interview questions

Basically there are two different types of interview questions that you could be asked. I will try to explain each of them and what they mean:

1.   Generic questions about you and your knowledge of the role and the Highways Agency.

Generic questions can be in any format. There is no particular structure to this type of question but they are generally far easier to respond to. Examples of generic questions would include:

- Why do you want to become a Traffic Officer?

- What has attracted you to this role in particular?

- What have you learnt about the role?

- Why should we choose you against the other applicants?

- What training will you undergo as a Traffic Officer?

2.   Role related questions.

This type of question is designed to assess your experience and skills in relation to the assessable qualities that are relevant to the role. Examples of role related questions include:

Q. Provide an example of where you have communicated effectively with a customer?

Q. Give an example of where you have taken responsibility to carry out a job or role to a high standard?

Q. Give an example of where you have taken pride in your delivery of work?

Q. Give an example of where you have provided exceptional customer care?

Q. Give an example of where you have worked with other people to achieve a common goal?

Q. Give an example of where you have carried out a safety related task or role?

Q. Give an example of where you have carried out a difficult task whilst under pressure?

On the following pages I have provided you with a number of sample interview questions and responses to assist you in your preparation. Please remember that the responses provided are not to be copied under any circumstances. Use them as a basis for your preparation taking examples from your own individual experiences and knowledge.

SAMPLE QUESTIONS AND RESPONSES

SAMPLE Q1
Why do you want to become a Traffic Officer?

This question is inevitable, so it is important that you ensure you have a suitable answer prepared. Many people will respond with a standard answer such as - "It's something that I've always wanted do since I was young". Whilst this is ok, you need to back it up with genuine reasons that relate to the role of a Traffic Officer and other important reasons such as working in a customer-focused environment and a desire to learn new skills.

This type of question may be posed in a number of different formats such as the following:

Q. Why do you want to become a Traffic Officer with the Highways Agency?

Q. What has attracted you to the role of Traffic Officer?

There now follows a sample response to help you prepare for this type of question. Once you have read it, use the template provided to create your own response based upon your own experiences and knowledge. Do not use any of the sample responses during your interview – make sure you create your own based on your own beliefs and circumstances.

SAMPLE RESPONSE
Why do you want to become a Traffic Officer?

"I have wanted to become a Traffic Officer for a number of years now and have been preparing for the role ever since. I have been very careful about making sure that this job is for me and that I am capable of meeting the high expectations of the role.

Apart from the fact that being a Traffic Officer is quite an exciting job, I also very much enjoy working with people and the challenges this can bring. I understand that as a Traffic Officer there are a lot of new skills to learn, especially during the early years. The type of person I am means that I would work hard to ensure that I passed every exam first time.

I also enjoy working in a customer-focused environment where a high level of service is essential. I understand that as a Traffic Officer I would be responsible for delivering a high quality service to the public and other agencies that you work with and I would enjoy the high level of responsibility that comes with the position."

TEMPLATE FOR SAMPLE QUESTION I
Why do you want to become a Traffic Officer?

SAMPLE Q2.

Why do you want to work for the Highways Agency?

Once again this is a question that is likely to come up during your interview. In order to prepare for this question, you need to carry out some research about the Highways Agency. The best place to get this information is via their website which can be found here:

http://www.highways.gov.uk

When responding to this type of question, try to focus on the positive aspects of the agencies work and what their mission/goals are. It is very important that you come across positive and provided genuine reasons for wanting to join them. Remember that they are committed to providing a high level of service and are determined to make our roads a safer place to travel.

There now follows a sample response to help you prepare for this type of question. Once you have read it, again use the template provided to create your own response based upon your own experiences and knowledge.

SAMPLE RESPONSE

Why do you want to work for the Highways Agency?

"Working for the Highways Agency has been an ambition of mine for a number of years now. I originally became interested in the organisation when a friend of mine was helped by a Traffic Officer after she broke down in her car on the motorway. She was very impressed with the help and assistance she received and it was from this point that I became interested in the role.

The Highways Agency has a very good reputation and I would enjoy working in such a positive team environment.

I am quite passionate about working in a customer focused role where there are challenges to deal with on a daily basis. The role of a Traffic Officer is one in which I believe I could make a positive contribution. I have studied the aims and objectives of the Highways Agency and I would like to help working towards them. I would also be very keen to learn the new skills required in order to become competent in the role.

I have a track record for being dedicated at work and have always passed work related tests and exams at the first attempt. I believe I have suitable skills and experience in order to meet the competencies that are relative to the role of a Traffic Officer and would make sure that I served the Highways Agency to the best of my ability."

TEMPLATE FOR SAMPLE QUESTION 2
Why do you want to work for the Highways Agency?

SAMPLE Q3
What can you tell us about the role of a Traffic Officer?

You must be well prepared for this question prior to your interview. If you don't know what the role involves, then you shouldn't be applying for the post. When responding to this question, make sure you make reference to the job/person specification for the role.

The job specification is a 'blueprint' for the role that you will be required to perform whilst working as a Highways Agency Traffic Officer. Therefore, it is essential that you know it. An example of a Traffic Officer's duties/person specification is detailed below:

MAIN RESPONSIBILITIES
- To provide the on-road resource to support the development of the Highways Agency's Network Operator Role.

- To reduce incident related congestion

- Managing collisions

- Removing damaged/ broken down and abandoned vehicles

- Clearing debris/ animals on carriageway

- To improve road safety for all road users

- Undertaking high visibility patrols

- Providing mobile/ temporary road closures

- Escorting or accompanying high risk, abnormal and other vehicles

- To improve journey time reliability

- Monitoring infrastructure and road works

- To improve customer relations

- Supporting special events

- Other duties

- Supporting crime management- working under Police direction and informing Police of road traffic offences and support enforcement

- Attending legal proceedings- give evidence as a witness

- Providing limited first aid when first on scene at an accident

SAMPLE RESPONSE
What can you tell us about the role of a Traffic Officer?

"The role of a Traffic Officer is predominantly based around the key core competencies of working with people, customer focus, communicating and influencing, working safely, problem solving, team working, decision making and finally working under pressure.

It is important that Traffic Officers are capable of applying these competencies whilst at work in order to carry out their role effectively. The role involves working towards reducing incident related congestion by managing collisions, removing damaged/ broken down and abandoned vehicles and clearing debris and animals on the carriageway.

Traffic Officers also have a responsibility to improve road safety for all road users and they achieve this by undertaking high visibility patrols, providing mobile and temporary road closures and escorting or accompanying high risk or abnormal vehicles.

In addition to the above key elements of the role Traffic Officers will also improve journey time reliability by monitoring infrastructure and road works and supporting special events. They can also be called upon to attend legal proceedings and give evidence as a witness and finally provide limited first aid when first on scene at an accident. Above all it is important that the role is carried out in accordance with procedures and also with a high degree of safety and competence."

Now use the blank template that follows to create your own response to this question.

TEMPLATE FOR SAMPLE QUESTION 3
What can you tell us about the role of a Traffic Officer?

SAMPLE Q4.
What skills do you possess that you think would be an asset to the Highways Agency team?

When responding to questions of this nature, try to match your skills with the skills that are required of a Traffic Officer. On the Highways Agency website, you will be able to see the type of person they are looking to employ. An example of this would be: 'We are looking for friendly, supportive people who share our professional, customer-focused approach. You must be a good team player with a flexible attitude and a willingness to learn.'

Just by looking at the Highway Agencies website, you should be able to obtain some clues as to the type of person they are seeking to employ. Try to think of the skills that are required to perform the role you are applying for and include them in your response. There now follows a sample response to this question. Once you have read it, take the time to construct your own response using the template provided.

SAMPLE RESPONSE
What skills do you possess that you think would be an asset to the Highways Agency team?

"I am a very conscientious person who takes the time to learn and develop new skills correctly. I have vast experience working in a customer-focused environment and fully understand that being able to deliver a high level of service is important. Without the customer there would be no company, so it is important that every member of the team works towards providing a high level of service. I believe I have the skills, knowledge and experience to be a competent and proficient Traffic Officer. I am a very good team player and can always be relied upon to carry out my role to the highest of standards. I am a flexible person and understand

how2become

that there is a need to be available at short notice to cover duties if required. In addition to these skills and attributes, I am a very good communicator and I am capable of working under pressure when required.

I have experience of having to communicate to customers in my previous role and believe that this would be an asset in the role of a Traffic Officer. I am highly safety conscious and have a health and safety qualification to my name. Therefore, I can be relied upon to perform all procedures relevant to the codes of conduct and will not put myself or others in any danger whatsoever. Finally, I am very good at learning new skills which means that I will work hard to pass all of my exams if I am successful in becoming a Traffic Officer."

TEMPLATE FOR SAMPLE QUESTION 4

What skills do you possess that you think would be an asset to the Highways Agency team?

SAMPLE Q5
Can you tell us about a situation when you have had to work under pressure?

The role of a Traffic Officer will sometimes involve a requirement to work under pressure. Therefore, the recruitment staff want to know that you have the ability to perform in such an environment. If you have experience of working under pressure then you are far more likely to succeed as a Traffic Officer.

When responding to a question of this nature, try to provide an actual specific example of where you have achieved a task whilst being under pressure. Questions of this nature are sometimes included in the Application Form, so try and use a different example for the Interview, if the question comes up. It would also be strongly advisable to use the S.T.A.R method when creating your response.

I have now provided a sample response to this question. Once you have read it, take the time to construct your own response based on your own individual experiences and knowledge using the template provided.

SAMPLE RESPONSE
Can you tell us about a situation when you have had to work under pressure?

"Yes, I can. In my current job as car mechanic for a well known company, I was presented with a difficult and pressurised situation. A member of the team had made a mistake and had fitted a number of wrong components to a car. The car in question was due to be picked up at 2pm and the customer had stated how important it was that his car was ready on time because he had an important meeting to attend.

We only had two hours in which to resolve the issue and I

volunteered to be the one who would carry out the work on the car. The problem was that we had 3 other customers in the workshop waiting for their cars too, so I was the only person who could be spared at that particular time. I worked solidly for the next 2 hours making sure that I meticulously carried out each task in line with our operating procedures. Even though I didn't finish the car until 2.10pm, I managed to achieve a very difficult task under pressurised conditions whilst keeping strictly to procedures and regulations."

TEMPLATE FOR SAMPLE QUESTION 5

Can you tell us about a situation when you have had to work under pressure?

SAMPLE Q6
Can you tell me when you have worked as part of a team to achieve a goal?

Having the ability to work as part of a team is very important to the role of a Traffic Officer. The Highways Agency employs many people in different roles from Regional Control Centre Operators to Highways Agency Records Officer. In fact there are many hundreds of people who work for the Highways Agency team. Therefore, it is essential that every member of the team works together in order to achieve the ultimate goal of providing a high quality service. The Highways Agency recruitment staff will want to be certain that you can work effectively as part of a team, which is why you may be asked questions that relate to your team-working experience.

There now follows a sample response to this question. Once you have read it, take time to construct your own response using the template provided.

SAMPLE RESPONSE
Can you tell me when you have worked as part of a team to achieve a goal?

"Yes, I can. I like to keep fit and healthy and as part of this aim I play football for a local Sunday team. We had worked very hard to get to the cup final and we were faced with playing a very good opposition team who had recently won the league title. After only ten minutes of play, one of our players was sent off and we conceded a penalty as a result. Being one goal down and 80 minutes left to play we were faced with a mountain to climb.

However, we all remembered our training and worked very hard in order to prevent any more goals being scored. Due to playing with ten players, I had to switch positions and play

as a defender, something that I am not used to. The team worked brilliantly to hold off any further opposing goals and after 60 minutes we managed to get an equaliser. The game went to penalties in the end and we managed to win the cup.

I believe I am an excellent team player and can always be relied upon to work as an effective team member at all times. I understand that being an effective team member is very important if the Highways Agency is to provide a high level of service to the road user. However, above all of this, effective teamwork is essential in order to maintain the high safety standards that are set in the role of a Traffic Officer."

TEMPLATE FOR SAMPLE QUESTION 6

Can you tell me when you have worked as part of a team to achieve a goal?

SAMPLE Q7
Can you provide us with an example of a safety-related task that you have had to perform?

Safety is an extremely important part of the Traffic Officer's role, and the recruitment staff need to know that you are capable of working safely at all times. The term 'safety' should be an integral part of your responses during the interview. Making reference to the fact that you are aware of the importance of safety at every opportunity is a positive thing.

When responding to safety-related questions, if they arise, try to include examples where you have had to work to, or follow, safety guidelines or procedures. If you have a safety qualification then it is definitely worthwhile mentioning this during your interview. Any relevant safety experience or related role should also be discussed. Now take a look at the following sample response before using the provided template to construct your own response.

SAMPLE RESPONSE
Can you provide us with an example of a safety-related task that you have had to perform?

"I currently work as a gas fitter and I am often required to perform safety-related tasks. An example of one of these tasks would involve the installation of gas-fired boilers. When fitting a gas boiler I have to ensure that I carry out a number of safety checks during the installation stage which ensures my work is safe and to a high standard. I have been trained, and I am qualified, to carry out my work in accordance with strict safety guidelines. I also have a number of safety certificates to demonstrate my competence.

I am fully aware that if I do not carry out my job in accordance

with safety guidelines there is the possibility that somebody may become injured or even killed."

TEMPLATE FOR SAMPLE QUESTION 7

Can you provide us with an example of a safety-related task that you have had to perform?

SAMPLE Q8
The role that you've applied for means that you'll be dealing with the safety of our customers and the delivery of our operation. Can you provide an example of how you have played a positive role as team member or leader?

Having the ability to work as an effective team member is important in any organisation and the Highways Agency are no exception. The Agency is made up of many different people, all of whom have an important role to perform. Therefore, it is essential that you have had some experience of working in a team environment, either as a team member or team leader. Remember that one of the assessable qualities requires you to take responsibility (leadership) for the delivery of your work. Try to think of an occasion when you have been part of a team or have even been the leader of a team. When responding to questions of this nature, think of a scenario where you worked as part of the team to achieve a task or solve a problem. Now take a look at the following sample response before using the template provided to construct your own.

SAMPLE RESPONSE
The role that you've applied for means that you'll be dealing with the safety of our customers and the delivery of our operation. Can you provide an example of how you have played a positive role as team member or leader?

"In my current role, I am responsible for the safety of my team and for ensuring that any health and safety incidents are reported in line with company regulations. I am also involved in coaching and mentoring my team and providing them with feedback, often helping them to improve. I currently lead a team of 18 staff and I am required to ensure the team operates effectively in terms of management, health

and safety, and training. Following any incident that relates to health and safety I always fully brief each member of the team to ensure that I have done everything in my power to prevent an incident occurring again."

TEMPLATE FOR SAMPLE QUESTION 8

The role that you've applied for means that you'll be dealing with the safety of our customers and the delivery of our operation. Can you provide an example of how you have played a positive role as team member or leader?

SAMPLE Q9
Part of the role of a Traffic Officer includes providing excellent customer service. What is the best example of customer service you have come across?

The majority of public services pride themselves on their high level of service and the Highways Agency is no different. It is essential that, during the Traffic Officer interview, you are able to provide at least one example of where you have provided excellent customer care. This type of question is designed to see how high your standards are, in relation to customer service. Those people who have a great deal of experience in a customer-focused environment will be able to answer this question with relative ease. However, those who have little experience in this area will need to spend more time preparing their response. Try to think of an occasion when you have witnessed an excellent piece of customer service and show that you learned from it. The question may also be posed in the following manner:

Q. Provide an example of where you have provided excellent customer service. What did you do and why?

Whatever response you provide, make sure it is unique and that it stands out. There now follows a sample response that relates to an individual who went that extra mile to make certain the customer was happy. Once you have read it, use the template that follows to create your own response based on your own experiences.

SAMPLE RESPONSE
Part of the role of a Traffic Officer includes providing excellent customer service. What is the best example of customer service you have come across?

"Whilst working as a shop assistant in my current role, a

member of the public came in to complain to the manager about a pair of football shoes that he had bought for his son's birthday. When his son came to open the present on the morning of his birthday, he noticed that one of the football boots was a larger size than the other. He was supposed to be playing football with his friends that morning and wanted to wear his new boots. However, due to the shop's mistake, this was not possible. Naturally, the boy was very upset. The manager of the shop was excellent in her approach to dealing with the situation. She remained calm throughout and listened to the gentleman very carefully, showing complete empathy for his son's situation. This immediately defused any potential confrontation. She then told him how sorry she was for the mistake that had happened, and that she would feel exactly the same if it was her own son who it had happened to. She then told the gentleman that she would refund the money in full and give his son a new pair of football boots to the same value as the previous pair. The man was delighted with her offer. Not only that, she then offered to give the man a further discount of 10% on any future purchase, due to the added inconvenience that was caused by him having to return to the shop to sort out the problem. I learned a lot from the way my manager dealt with this situation. She used exceptional communication skills and remained calm throughout. She then went the extra mile to make the gentleman's journey back to the shop a worthwhile one.

The potential for losing a customer was averted by her actions and I feel sure the man would return to our shop again."

TEMPLATE FOR SAMPLE QUESTION 9

Part of the role of a Traffic Officer includes providing excellent customer service. What is the best example of customer service you have come across?

10. What is your sickness record like and what do you think is an acceptable level of sickness?

Most employers detest sickness and they especially detest sickness that is not genuine. For every day that an employee is off sick will cost the Highways Agency dearly. Therefore, they want to employ people who have good sickness records.

Obviously you cannot lie when responding to this question as the Highways Agency will carry out checks. The latter part of the question is simple to answer. Basically no amount of sickness is acceptable but sometimes genuine sickness cannot be helped.

Remember to tell them that you do not take time off sick unless absolutely necessary and you can be relied upon to come to work.

11. Have you ever worked during the night and how do you feel about working shifts?

The role of a Traffic Officer involves irregular shifts and the Highways Agency want to know that you can handle them. Speak to any person who works shifts and they will tell you that after a number of years they can start to take their toll. Remember to tell the panel that you are looking forward to working shifts and, in particular, night duties. If you can provide examples of where you have worked irregular shift patterns then remember to tell them.

12. What are the mission and aims of the Highways Agency?

Many organisations, including the Highways Agency set themselves aims and objectives. They usually relate to the high level of customer service that they promise to deliver.

 how2become

When you apply to become a Traffic Officer you should not only prepare for each stage of the selection process but you should also learn as much as possible about the Agency you are applying to join.

Learning this kind of information is important and it will demonstrate your seriousness about joining their particular company. Always remember this rule – Working for the Highways Agency comes first, becoming a Traffic Officer comes second! Visit the website of the Highways Agency in order to view their mission, aims, objectives or customer charter.

http://www.highways.gov.uk

13. Can you provide us with an example of when you have had to work in an emergency?

Being able to remain calm under pressure is very important and will form an integral part of your training. Maybe you have had to deal with an emergency at work or even in the home?

Whatever example you decide to use, make sure you tell them that you stayed calm and focused on the task in hand. Make reference to the importance of safety during your response too.

14. Do you think it's important for Traffic Officers to wear a uniform?

The answer to this question should be yes - providing that is your honest belief. The reason for this is that a uniform gives road user's confidence in the service they are receiving. It is also important during an emergency situation so that road users know who to turn to for help and guidance. Uniforms are positive for the image of Traffic Officer which is why the

Highways Agency uses them. Be positive about uniforms and tell them that you are looking forward to wearing one and taking pride in your appearance.

QUESTIONS BASED AROUND THE ASSESSABLE COMPETENCIES

At the beginning of this guide I made reference to the assessable competencies. I can almost guarantee that you'll be asked a number of interview questions that are centred around these important areas. Although I have covered a number of the competencies in some of the interview questions provided within this section already, it is important to cover each assessable area, and more importantly, provide you wit some sample questions to assist you in your preparation.

Communicates well with others (Communicating and Marketing)
Sample questions:

Q. Provide an example of where you have communicated a difficult message to a group of people.

Q. Provide an example of where you have had to direct people during an emergency situation.

Q. Provide an example of where you have had to communicate a sensitive message to somebody. What did you say and why?

Q. When communicating a message to a group of people, what factors would you take into account?

Taking responsibility for, and pride in, the delivery of your own work (Leadership)

Q. Provide an example of where you have taken responsibility for a task.

Q. Provide an example of where you have acted as a role model to other people.

Q. What would you do if a member of your team was not pulling his/her own weight?

Q. If you were given a difficult task to carry out at work, how would you make sure that the task was carried out responsibly and to a high standard?

Providing the best quality service to our customers (Customer service)

Q. Give an example of where you have delivered excellent customer service.

Q. Why do you think we place so much emphasis on excellent customer service?

Q. What is our customer promise?

Q. Give an example of where you have had to deal with a customer complaint? What did you do and how did you resolve the complaint?

Q. Whilst working as a Traffic Officer you come across a broken down vehicle. After stopping to assist the driver, he quickly becomes aggressive and confrontational. How would you deal with this situation?

Working with other teams, organisations and the public (Partnership Working and Stakeholder Management

Q. Give an example of where you have worked with other people/organisations to achieve a common goal.

Q. Whilst working as a team member, what factors would you take into consideration?

Q. What are the elements of good team work?

Ensuring safety of yourself, colleagues and the public (Safety)
Q. Give an example of a safety related role that you have carried out.

Q. Give an example of where you have had to follow rules and procedures at work.

Q. What would you do if you came across an unsafe working practice whilst on duty as a Traffic Officer?

Working under pressure to manage incidents and conflict (Incident Management)
Q. How do you cope with pressure?

Q. Give an example of where you have carried out a difficult task whilst under strict time constraints.

FURTHER POSSIBLE INTERVIEW QUESTIONS

- What has attracted you to the role of a Traffic Officer?

- What do you think you could bring to the role?

- What are your strengths?

- What are your weaknesses?

- Why do you want to leave your current employment?

- What qualities do you think are needed to become a Traffic Officer?

- What can you tell me about the Highways Agency?

- What have you done to prepare yourself for this position?

- Can you provide an example of where you have worked in a customer focused role?

- Can you tell us what skills and experience you can bring to this role?

- Can you provide an example of where you have recently had to learn a new skill?

- Can you provide an example of where you have worked in a safety critical role?

TIPS FOR PASSING TRAFFIC OFFICER INTERVIEW

Competency based interview questions are usually used by the Highways Agency when selecting Traffic Officers. This type of interview is slightly different to the style you may be used to. A 'normal' interview will usually consist of questions such as:

"Tell us why you want this post?"

"What do you have to offer?"

"Why have you applied for this position?"

The above type of interview questions should still form part of your preparation but it is very important that you also prepare for competency based questions such as:

"Please provide us with an example of when..." or *"Please describe a situation when"* etc.

Because the style of interview will involve 'competency' based questions it is essential that you learn and understand the competencies that are relevant to this role. The competencies that form part of the Traffic Officers role are as follows:

- Working with people

- Customer focus

- Communicating and influencing

- Problem solving and decision making

- Working under pressure

The first part of your preparation for the Traffic officer interview is to try and think of specific situations that you have experienced where you have experienced the above competencies.

The questions could be presented in the following format:

"Can you provide an example of where you have had to work with other people as part of a team in order to achieve a common goal?"

"Please provide us with an example of where you have delivered a high level of service"

"Have you ever had to solve a difficult problem?"

"Please provide us with an example of where you have had to make a difficult decision despite opposition from others"

"Have you ever had to work under pressure to achieve a difficult task?"

The above questions could be presented in many different forms but in order to prepare for the competency based interview questions effectively you must try to think of specific examples of where you can meet the competencies.

CONSTRUCTING YOUR RESPONSES TO THE INTERVIEW QUESTIONS

It is important that you responses are specific and also that they follow a logical order. You may wish to use the S.T.A.R method when constructing your responses in order to make them flow better and also to ensure they meet the required criteria.

Remember that S.T.A.R stands for:

SPECIFIC

TASK

ACTION

RESULT

Try to make sure your responses end on a positive note and the result is one that achieved the task.

PROBING QUESTIONS

Some competency based interviews can involve what are more commonly known as 'probing' questions. A probing question is designed to allow the interviewer to find out more about the situation that you are describing. Examples of probing questions are as follows:

"How did that make you feel?"

"What did the others think of your decision?"

"Would you have done anything different next time?"

"What, if anything, did you learn from the experience?"

"Did you encounter any problems or pitfalls and if so how did you overcome them"

WHAT ARE THE INTERVIEWERS LOOKING FOR?

I can not overemphasis enough that the interview panel will be looking for specific examples about exactly what you did in these situations. Do not be generic in your responses as these will not score high. You can use relevant examples from your current job, a previous role, or a situation outside of work altogether such as your personal life. You will be asked to discuss the example in some detail so make sure you are honest and also that you know the situation or example inside out!

The interviewers will also want to ask you questions about the information you have provided in your application form so make sure you take a copy of it before you submit it and also read it before your interview.

CHAPTER 7
HOW TO GET
TRAFFIC OFFICER FIT

INTRODUCTION

Within this guide I have provided you with a number of useful exercises that will allow you to prepare for the role of a Traffic Officer and assist you in your preparation for the medical. Whilst there is not normally a fitness assessment that forms part of the selection process, it is important that you are physically fit and healthy. You will need to pass a thorough medical before you are accepted.

Traffic Officers need to have a good all-round aerobic fitness and also a good level of strength and stamina. The exercises contained within this guide will help you to achieve exactly that. Do not spend hours in the gym lifting heavy weights as the job does not require that level of strength, but rather aim for a varied and diverse fitness programme that covers exercises such as swimming, rowing, jogging, brisk walking and light weight work.

In addition to getting/keeping fit, keep an eye on your diet and try to eat healthy foods whilst drinking plenty of water. It will all go a long way to helping you improve your general well-being and concentration levels whilst you prepare for the selection process.

PLANNING YOUR WORKOUTS IN PREPARATION FOR THE MEDICAL

Most people who embark on a fitness regime in January have given it up by February. The reason why most people give up their fitness regime so soon is mainly due to a lack of proper preparation. Throughout the duration of the selection process you need to focus on preparation, and the same word applies when preparing for the medical. Preparation is key to your success and it is essential that you plan your workouts effectively.

To begin with, try to think about the role of a Traffic Officer and what it entails. Although the majority of work that you carry out will be sat in a vehicle, it is crucially important that your concentration levels are at their peak. You can achieve this by carrying out a varied and consistent fitness training programme. In the build-up to the selection process and the medical, I advise that you concentrate on specific exercises that will allow you to perform to your optimum. Read on for some great ways to stay fit all year round.

Get an assessment before you start training

The first step is to get a fitness test at the gym, weigh yourself and run your fastest mile. Once you have done all three of these you should write down your results and keep them hidden away somewhere safe. After a month of following your new fitness regime, do all three tests again and check your results against the previous month's. This is a great way

to monitor your performance and progress and it will also keep you motivated and focused on your goals.

Keep a check on what you eat and drink

Make sure you write down everything you eat and drink for a whole week. You must include tea, water, milk, biscuits and anything and everything that you digest. You will soon begin to realise how much you are eating and you will notice areas in which you can make some changes. For example, if you are taking sugar with your tea then why not try reducing it or giving it up altogether. If you do then you will soon notice the difference.

It is important that you start to look for opportunities to improve your fitness and well-being right from the offset. These areas are what I call 'easy wins'.

Exercises that will help you to stay fit and prepare effectively for the medical

It is my strong belief that you do not have to attend a gym in order to prepare for the Traffic Officer medical. If I was applying to become a Traffic Officer today then I would embark on a fitness programme that included brisk walking, running, rowing, press-ups, sit-ups, squats and lunges. In order to improve my upper body strength I would also go swimming.

Walking is one of the best exercises you can do as part of your preparation for the Traffic Officer medical. Whilst it shouldn't be the only form of exercise you carry out, it will go a long way to improving your focus and general well-being. Now when I say 'walking' I don't mean a gentle stroll, I mean 'brisk' walking. Try walking at a fast pace for 30 minutes every day for a 7-day period. Then see how you feel at the end of the 7 days. I guarantee you'll begin to feel a lot healthier

and fitter. Brisk walking is also a fantastic way to lose weight if you think you need to. In addition to helping you to lose weight it will also keep your concentration and motivational levels up.

There are some more great exercises contained within this guide and most of them can be carried out without the need to attend a gym.

One step at a time

Only you will know how fit you are. I advise that you first of all write down the areas that you believe or feel you need to improve on. For example, if you feel that you need to work on your upper body strength then pick out exercises from this guide that will work on that area for you.

The key to making improvements is to do it gradually, and at one step at a time. Try to set yourself small goals. If you think you need to lose two stone in weight then focus on losing a few pounds at a time. For example, during the first month aim to lose 6 pounds only. Once you have achieved this then again aim to lose 6 pounds over the next month, and so on and so forth. The more realistic your goal, the more likely you are to achieve it. One of the biggest problems people encounter when starting a fitness regime is that they become bored quickly. This then leads to a lack of motivation and desire, and soon the fitness programme stops.

Change your exercise routine often. Instead of walking try jogging. Instead of jogging try cycling with the odd day of swimming. Keep your workouts varied and interesting to ensure that you stay focused and motivated.

STRETCHING

How many people stretch before carrying out any form of

exercise? Very few people, is the correct answer! Not only is it irresponsible but it is also placing you at high risk from injury. Before we commence with the exercises we will take a look at a few warm-up stretches. Make sure you stretch fully before carrying out any exercises. You want your career as a Traffic Officer to be a long one and that means looking after yourself, including stretching! It is also very important to check with your GP that you are medically fit to carry out any form of physical exercise.

The warm-up calf stretch

To perform this stretch effectively you should first of all start off by facing a wall whilst standing upright. Your right foot should be close to the wall and your right knee bent. Now place your hands flat against the wall and at a height that is level with your shoulders. Stretch your left leg far out behind you, without lifting your toes and heel off the floor, and lean towards the wall.

Once you have performed this stretch for 25 seconds, switch legs and carry out the same procedure for the right leg. As with all exercises contained within this guide, stop if you feel any pain or discomfort.

Stretching the shoulder muscles

To begin with, stand with your feet slightly apart and with your knees only slightly bent. Now hold your arms right out in front of you, with your palms facing away from you and with your fingers pointing skywards. Now place your right palm on the back of your left hand and use it to push the left hand further away from you. If you are performing this exercise correctly then you will feel the muscles in your shoulder stretching. Hold for 10 seconds before switching sides.

Stretching the quad muscles (front of the thigh)

Before you carry out any form of brisk walking or running, it is imperative that you stretch your leg muscles. To begin with, stand with your right hand pressed against the back of a wall or firm surface. Bend your left knee and bring your left heel up to your bottom whilst grasping your foot with your left hand. Your back should be straight and your shoulders, hips and knees should all be in line at all times during the exercise. Hold for 25 seconds before switching legs.

Stretching the hamstring muscles (back of the thigh)

To perform this exercise correctly, stand up straight and place your right foot onto a table or other firm surface so that your leg is almost parallel to the floor. Keep your left leg straight and your foot at a right angle to your leg. Start to slowly move your hands down your right leg towards your ankle until you feel tension on the underside of your thigh. When you feel this tension you know that you are starting to stretch the hamstring muscles. Hold for 25 seconds before switching legs.

We have only covered a small number of stretching exercises within this section; however, it is crucial that you stretch out fully in all areas before carrying out any of the following exercises. Remember to obtain professional advice before carrying out any type of exercise.

RUNNING

As I have already mentioned, one of the best ways to prepare for the Traffic Officer medical is to embark on a structured running programme. You do not need to run at a fast pace or even run for long distances, in order to gain massively from this type of exercise.

Before I joined the Fire Service I spent a few years in the Royal Navy. I applied to join the Navy when I was 16 and I made it through the selection process with ease until I reached the medical. During the medical the doctor told me that I was overweight and that I had to lose a stone before they would accept me. To be honest, I was heartbroken. I couldn't believe it; especially after all the hard work I had put in preparing for the tests and the interview! Anyway, as soon as I arrived back home from the medical I started out on a structured running programme that would see me lose the stone in weight within only 4 weeks! The following running programme is very similar to the one I used all those years ago and it will serve you well when preparing for the fitness tests.

Before I provide you with the running programme, however, take a read of the following important running tips.

Tips for running

- As with any exercise, you should consult a doctor before taking part to make sure that you are medically fit.

- It is certainly worth investing in a pair of comfortable running shoes that serve the purpose for your intended training programme. Your local sports shop will be able to advise you on the types that are best for you. You don't have to spend a fortune to buy a good pair of running shoes.

- It is a good idea to invest in a 'high visibility' jacket or coat so that you can be seen by fast moving traffic if you intend to run on or near the road.

- Make sure you carry out at least 5 whole minutes of stretching exercises not only before but also after your running programme. This can help to prevent injury.

- Whilst you shouldn't run on a full stomach, it is also not good to run on an empty one either. A great food to eat approximately 30 minutes before a run is a banana. This is great for giving you energy.

- Drink plenty of water throughout the day. Try to drink at least 1.5 litres each day in total. This will keep you hydrated and help to prevent muscle cramp.

- Don't overdo it. If you feel any pain or discomfort then stop and seek medical advice.

RUNNING PROGRAMME WEEK 1

DAY 1
- Run a total of 3 miles only at a steady pace.

If you cannot manage 3 miles then try the following:

- Walk at a brisk pace for half a mile or approximately 10 minutes.

Then

- Run for 1 mile or 8 minutes.

Then

- Walk for another half a mile or approximately 10 minutes.

Then

- Run for 1.5 miles or 12 minutes.

Walking at a brisk pace is probably the most effective way to lose weight if you need to. It is possible to burn the same amount of calories if you walk the same distance as if you were running.

When walking at a 'brisk' pace it is recommended that you

walk as fast as is comfortably possible without breaking into a run or slow jog.

DAY 2
- Walk for 2 miles or approximately 20 minutes at a brisk pace.

Then

- Run for 2 miles or 14 minutes.

DAY 3
- Repeat DAY ONE.

DAY 4
- Walk at a brisk pace for 0.5 miles or approximately 7 minutes.

Then

- Run for 3 miles or 20 minutes.

DAY 5
- Repeat DAY ONE.

DAY 6 AND DAY 7
- Rest days. No exercise.

RUNNING PROGRAMME WEEK 2

DAY 1
- Run for 4 miles or 25 minutes.

DAY 2
- Run a total of 3 miles at a steady pace.

If you cannot manage 3 miles then try the following:

- Walk at a brisk pace for half a mile or approximately 10 minutes.

Then

- Run for 1 mile or 8 minutes.

Then

- Walk for another half a mile or approximately 10 minutes.

Then

- Run for 1.5 miles or 12 minutes.

DAY 3
- Rest day. No exercise.

DAY 4
- Run for 5 miles or 35 to 40 minutes.

DAY 5
- Run for 3 miles or 20 minutes.

Then

- Walk at a brisk pace for 2 miles or approximately 20 minutes.

DAY 6
- Run for 5 miles or 35 to 45 minutes.

DAY 7
- Rest day. No exercise.

Once you have completed the second week running programme, use the third week to perform different types of exercises, such as cycling and swimming. During week 4 you can then commence the 2-week running programme again. You'll be amazed at how much easier it is the second

time around!

When preparing for the selection process, use your exercise time as a break from your studies. For example, if you have been working on the application form for a couple of hours why not take a break and go running? When you return from your run you can then concentrate on your studies feeling refreshed.

Now that I've provided you with a structured running programme to follow, there really are no excuses. So, get out there and start running! I'll now provide you with a number of key targeted exercises that will allow you to improve your all-round fitness, stamina and concentration levels in preparation for the Traffic Officer selection process and medical.

EXERCISES THAT WILL IMPROVE YOUR FITNESS, STAMINA AND CONCENTRATION LEVELS

Press-ups

Whilst running is a great way to improve your overall fitness, you may also decide to carry out exercises that improve your upper body strength. Press-ups are ideal for improving upper body strength and you don't have to attend a gym to perform them.

However, you must ensure that you can do them correctly as injury can occur. You only need to spend just 5 minutes every day on press-ups, possibly after you go running or even before if you prefer. If you are not used to doing press-ups then start slowly and aim to carry out at least 10.

Even if you struggle to do just 10, you will soon find that after a few days' practice at these you will be up to 20+.

Step 1 - To begin with, lie on a mat or even surface. Your hands should be shoulder width apart and your arms fully extended.

Step 2 - Gradually lower your body until the elbows reach 90°. Do not rush the movement as you may cause injury.

Step 3 - Once your elbows reach 90° slowly return to the starting position with your arms fully extended.

The press-up action should be a continuous movement with no rest. However, it is important that the exercise is as smooth as possible and there should be no jolting or sudden movements. Try to complete as many press-ups as possible and always keep a record of how many you do. This will keep you focused and also maintain your motivation levels.

Did you know that the world record for non-stop press-ups is currently 10,507 set in 1980!

WARNING – Ensure you take advice from a competent fitness trainer in relation to the correct execution of press-up exercises and other exercises contained within this guide.

Sit-ups
Sit-ups are great for building the core stomach muscles. At the commencement of the exercise lie flat on your back with your knees bent at a 45° angle and with your feet together. Your hands can either be crossed on your chest, by your sides, or cupped behind your ears.

Without moving your lower body, curl your upper torso upwards and in towards your knees, until your shoulder blades are as high off the ground as possible. As you reach the highest point, tighten your abdominal muscles for a brief second. This will allow you to get the most out of the exercise. Now slowly start to lower yourself back to the

starting position. You should be aiming to work up to at least 50 effective sit-ups every day. You will be amazed at how quickly this can be achieved and you will begin to notice your stomach muscles developing.

Pull-ups

Pull-ups are another great way for building the core upper body muscle groups. The unfortunate thing about this type of exercise is you will probably need to attend a gym in order to carry them out. Having said that, there are a number of different types of 'pull-up bars' available to buy on the market that can easily and safely be fitted to a doorway at home. If you choose to purchase one of these items make sure that it conforms to the relevant safety standards first.

Lateral pull-ups are very effective at increasing upper body strength. If you have access to a gymnasium then these can be practised on a 'lateral pull-up' machine. It is advised that you consult a member of staff at your gym to ask about these exercises.

Pull-ups should be performed by firmly grasping a sturdy and solid bar. Before you grasp the bar make sure it is safe. Your hands should be roughly shoulder-width apart. Straighten your arms so that your body hangs loose. You will feel your lateral muscles and biceps stretching as you hang in the air. This is the starting position for the lateral pull-up exercise.

Next, pull yourself upwards to the point where your chest is almost touching the bar and your chin is actually over the bar. Whilst pulling upwards, focus on keeping your body straight without any arching or swinging as this can result in injury. Once your chin is over the bar, you can lower yourself back down to the initial starting position. Repeat the exercise 10 times.

Squats (these work the legs and bottom)

Squats are a great exercise for working the leg muscles. They are the perfect exercise for improving your general fitness and stamina levels.

At the commencement of the exercise, stand up straight with your arms at your sides. Concentrate on keeping your feet shoulder-width apart and your head up. Do not look downwards at any point during the exercise. You will see from the picture above that the person has their lower back slightly arched. They are also holding light weights, which can add to the intensity of the exercise.

Now start to very slowly bend your knees while pushing your rear out as though you are about to sit down on a chair. Keep lowering yourself down until your thighs reach past the 90° point. Make sure your weight is on your heels so that your knees do not extend over your toes. At this point you may wish to tighten your thighs and buttocks to intensify the exercise.

As you come back up to a standing position, push down through your heels, which will allow you to maintain your balance. Repeat the exercise 15 to 20 times.

Lunges (these work the thighs and bottom)

You will have noticed throughout this section of the guide that I have been providing you with simple, yet highly effective exercises that can be carried out at home. The lunge exercise is another great addition to the range of exercises that require no attendance at the gym.

To begin with, stand with your back straight and your feet together (you may hold light hand weights if you wish to add some intensity to the exercise).

Next, take a big step forward, making sure you inhale as

go and landing with the heel first. Bend the front knee no more than 90 degrees so as to avoid injury. Keep your back straight and lower the back knee as close to the floor as possible. Your front knee should be lined up over your ankle and your back thigh should be in line with your back.

To complete the exercise, exhale and push down against your front heel, squeezing your buttocks tight as you rise back to the starting position.

Try to repeat the exercise 15 to 20 times before switching sides.

Lateral raises (these work the shoulder muscles)
Whilst Traffic Officers are not usually required to lift heavy items of equipment during their day-to-day work, they still need to have a good level of upper body strength. Lateral raises will allow you to improve your upper body strength in a safe and effective manner.

Take a dumbbell in each hand and hold them by the sides of your body with your palms facing inwards.

Stand or sit with your feet shoulder-width apart, knees slightly bent. Do not lean backwards as you could cause injury to your back. Raise your arms up and out to the sides until they are parallel to the ground, then lower them back down carefully. Repeat the exercise 15 to 20 times.

ALTERNATIVE EXERCISES

Swimming
Apart from press-ups, lateral raises and the other exercises I have provided you with, another fantastic way to improve your upper body and overall fitness is to go swimming. If you have access to a swimming pool, and you can swim, then

this is a brilliant way to improve your fitness.

If you are not a great swimmer you can start off with short distances and gradually build up your swimming strength and stamina. Breaststroke is sufficient for building good upper body strength providing you put the effort into swimming an effective number of lengths. You may wish to alternate your running programme with the odd day of swimming. If you can swim 10 lengths of a 25-metre pool initially then this is a good base to start from. You will soon find that you can increase this number easily providing that you carry on swimming every week. Try running to your local swimming pool, if it is not too far away, swimming 20 lengths of breaststroke, and then running back home.

This is a great way to combine your fitness activity and prevent yourself from becoming bored of your training programme.

Rowing

If there is one exercise that will allow you to work every single muscle group in the body then it is rowing. It will increase your aerobic fitness and it will also improve your lower and upper body strength. As with any exercise of this nature there is a risk of injury. It is crucial that you use the correct technique when rowing on a purpose-built machine. By applying the correct technique you will be far more efficient and you will also see faster results.

Whilst exercising on the rowing machine, make sure you keep your back straight and concentrate on using your legs and buttocks. Never extend so far that you lock out your knees. Try to be smooth throughout the entire exercise. To obtain a suitable indoor rowing training programme that is relevant to your current fitness levels please visit www.concept2.co.uk.

TIPS FOR STAYING WITH YOUR WORKOUT

The hardest part of your training programme will be sticking with it. In this final section of your fitness guide I will provide some useful golden rules that will enable you to maintain your motivational levels in the build-up to the Traffic Officer selection process. In order to stay with your workout for longer, try following these simple rules:

Golden rule number one - Work out often
Aim to train three to five times each and every week.

Each training session should last between 20 minutes to a maximum of an hour. The quality of training is important so don't go for heavy weights but instead go for a lighter weight with a better technique. On days when you are feeling energetic, take advantage of this opportunity and do more!

Within this guide I have deliberately provided you with a number of 'simple-to-perform' exercises that are targeted at the core muscle groups required to maintain a good level of physical fitness. In between your study sessions try carrying out these exercises at home or get yourself out on the road running or cycling. Use your study 'down-time' effectively and wisely.

Golden rule number two - Mix up your exercises
Your exercise programme should include some elements of cardiovascular (aerobics, running, brisk walking and cycling), resistance training (weights or own body exercises such as press-ups and sit-ups) and, finally, flexibility (stretching). Make sure that you always warm up and warm down.

If you are a member of a gym then consider taking up a

class such as Pilates. This form of exercise class will teach you how to build core training into your exercise principles, and show you how to hit your abdominals in ways that are not possible with conventional sit-ups. If you are a member of a gym then a fantastic 'all-round' exercise that I strongly recommend is rowing. Rowing will hit every major muscle group in your body and it is also perfect for improving your stamina levels and cardiovascular fitness.

Golden rule number three - Eat a healthy and balanced diet

It is vitally important that you eat the right fuel to give you the energy to train to your full potential. Don't fill your body with rubbish and then expect to train well. Think about what you are eating and drinking, including the quantities, and keep a record of what you are digesting. You will become stronger and fitter more quickly if you eat little amounts of nutritious foods at short intervals.

Golden rule number four - Get help

Try working with a personal trainer. They will ensure that you work hard and will help you to achieve your goals. If you cannot afford a personal trainer then try training with some-one else. The mere fact that they are there at your side will add an element of competition to your training sessions!

A consultation with a professional nutritionist will also help you improve your eating habits and establish your individual food needs.

Golden rule number five - Fitness is for life

One of my old managers in the Fire Service had a saying – "Fitness Wins!" Two simple words that meant an awful lot! Improving your fitness and eating healthily are not short-term projects. They are things that should come naturally to you.

Make fitness a permanent part of your life by following these tips, and you'll lead a better and more fulfilling life!

Good luck and work hard to improve your weak areas.

A FEW FINAL WORDS

You have now reached the end of the guide and no doubt you will be ready to start preparing for the Traffic Officer selection process. Just before you go off and start on your preparation, consider the following.

The majority of candidates who pass the Traffic Officer selection process have a number of common attributes. These are as follows:

They believe in themselves
Regardless of what anyone tells you, you can become a Traffic Officer. Just like any job of this nature, you have to be prepared to work hard in order to be successful. Make sure you have the self-belief to pass the selection process, match each and every one of the assessable qualities, and also fill your mind with positive thoughts.

They prepare fully
Those people who achieve in life prepare fully for every eventuality and that is what you must do when you apply to become a Traffic Officer. Work very hard and especially concentrate on your weak areas.

They persevere
Perseverance is a fantastic word. Everybody comes across obstacles or setbacks in their life, but it is what you do about those setbacks that is important. If you fail at something, then ask yourself 'why' you have failed. This will allow you to improve for next time and if you keep improving and trying, success will eventually follow. Apply this same method of thinking when you apply to become a Traffic Officer.

They are self-motivated
How much do you want this job? Do you want it, or do you

really want it?

When you apply to join the Highways Agency you should want it more than anything in the world. Your levels of self-motivation will shine through on your application and during your interview. For the weeks and months leading up to the Traffic Officer selection process, be motivated as best you can and always keep your fitness levels up as this will serve to increase your levels of motivation.

Work hard, stay focused and be what you want…

Richard McMunn

how2become

Visit www.how2become.co.uk to find more titles and courses that will help you to pass Traffic Officer selection process, including:

- How to pass the Traffic Officer interview DVD.

- 1 Day Traffic Officer training course.

- Psychometric testing books and CD's.

www.how2become.co.uk